I0416980

Stormwater

to

Street Trees:

Engineering Urban Forests for

Stormwater Management

U.S. Environmental Protection Agency

Office of Wetlands, Oceans and Watersheds

Nonpoint Source Control Branch (4503T)

1200 Pennsylvania Ave., NW

Washington, DC 20460

September 2013

EPA 841-B-13-001

Mention of trade names, products, or services does not convey official EPA approval, endorsement, or recommendation.

Table of Contents

Acknowledgements

The U.S. Environmental Protection Agency would like to acknowledge the many individual and organizational researchers, government employees, and consultants whose efforts helped bring this guide to fruition.

This guide, *Stormwater to Street Trees: Engineering Urban Forests for Stormwater Management*, was developed by the office of Office of Wetlands, Oceans and Watersheds, Nonpoint Source Control Branch (4503T) of the U.S. Environmental Protection Agency. Chris Solloway managed the overall development of this guide. Lisa Hair provided content and technical and editorial support for the entire document.

A team of urban foresters, arborists, and planners from Davey Resource Group, a division of The Davey Tree Expert Company, developed *Stormwater to Street Trees: Engineering Urban Forests for Stormwater Management* for the U.S Environmental Protection Agency through research and analysis and discussions with the users of the engineered systems presented in this guide. The Davey Resource Group team included Tina McKeand and Shirley Vaughn who co-authored this guide; Tina McKeand also created the graphics. Chad Clink, Andrew Hillman, and Ruth Ann Sobnosky helped Tina and Shirley research and provided support services throughout the project.

Introduction

The presence of trees in a streetscape, neighborhood, and community can decrease the amount of stormwater runoff and pollutants that reach local waters.

❖ Trees reduce stormwater runoff by capturing and storing rainfall in their canopy and releasing water into the atmosphere.

❖ Tree roots and leaf litter create soil conditions that promote the infiltration of rainwater into the soil.

❖ Trees help slow down and temporarily store runoff and reduce pollutants by taking up nutrients and other pollutants from soils and water through their roots.

❖ Trees transform pollutants into less harmful substances.

Trees are natural managers of stormwater. When included as part of a system engineered to manage stormwater, they can improve infiltration and capacity, reducing the overall amount of runoff. Photo courtesy of Davey Resource Group.

Cities employ a variety of measures to manage stormwater runoff. However, most do not take advantage of the stormwater utility benefits trees provide. Grey stormwater systems use curbs, gutters, drains, pipes, ponds, vaults, and outfalls to move water quickly to containment and/or treatment areas or to receiving waters. Alternatively, green stormwater systems manage stormwater on site with overflow ability, creating areas that mimic nature. Vegetation, swales, wetlands, buffer zones, and pervious surfaces capture, filter, and slow stormwater runoff. Volume is managed through evapotranspiration, infiltration, and soil moisture recharge.

Stormwater is a problem for cities across the country. Existing grey and green stormwater management systems are often not enough to accommodate runoff. Adding trees to those systems is a cost-effective way to improve their function and reduce runoff. Photo courtesy of Davey Resource Group.

Trees are typically not considered part of either grey or green stormwater management systems; they are generally, and falsely, considered to be of landscaping value. Planting a tree just for landscaping is not taking advantage of the stormwater utility benefits and other environmental services it provides.

In urban areas, trees are part of the managed municipal infrastructure. A street tree, which is generally a publicly managed tree found growing within the right-of-way, offers unique opportunities to increase the effectiveness of grey and green stormwater systems.

With urbanization on the rise and impervious surfaces dominating urban cores, existing stormwater and sewer systems are often inadequate to handle peak flows. When a system is overtaxed, peak flows can blow manhole covers from the ground and back up stormwater and, in some cases, even sewage into the streets. To reduce pressure on existing systems and increase capacity, cities must consider every available option, especially using trees, to help manage stormwater.

Installing trees in locations that are engineered to retain stormwater is a great way to augment existing stormwater management systems, increasing their capacity and improving water quality while greatly improving urban forest canopy. This guide is an introduction to those engineered systems available, and in use today, that utilize trees to manage a volume of stormwater. These systems, in addition to providing a solution for managing runoff, also grow big trees.

USING THIS GUIDE

This guide is divided into the following four sections:

Section 1. Urban Stormwater Runoff defines urban stormwater runoff and explains why it is a problem.

Section 2. The Role of Trees in Stormwater Management discusses what trees need to grow in urban environments and how they help manage stormwater.

Section 3. Stormwater Management Systems with Trees provides an introduction to engineered systems available that utilize trees to manage a volume of stormwater.

Section 4. Case Studies presents projects from throughout the country that have successfully used trees in the engineered systems discussed.

This guide is intended to help engineers, planners, developers, architects, arborists, and public officials understand how trees perform and interact in a stormwater management system, and the new technologies that are being used to increase the stormwater utility function of the urban forest, even in the densest urban environments.

The illustrations in this guide are not intended to serve as construction drawings. They should be used to communicate concepts about how properly designed urban tree systems help reduce stormwater runoff, while concurrently improving tree health.

Although each system is presented independently, a combination of systems uniquely designed for a specific site will provide the greatest benefits.

Because every project and installation is different, appropriate consideration of the ecoregion, site, and project goals are a must for a successful outcome.

Always consult with regulatory bodies, engineers, arborists, planners, landscape architects, and other stakeholders to ensure development plans and project implementation meet site needs as well as all local, state, and federal regulations and requirements regarding the capture, detainment, storage, and/or manipulation of stormwater runoff.

Section 1. Urban Stormwater Runoff

By design and function, urban areas are covered with impervious surfaces such as roofs, streets, sidewalks, and parking lots. All of those surfaces contribute to urban stormwater runoff which is caused when precipitation from rain and snowmelt flows over land and impervious surfaces without infiltrating the ground. Stormwater runoff is a problem for everyone.

WHY IS URBAN STORMWATER RUNOFF A PROBLEM?

As stormwater flows over city streets and sidewalks and through parking lots, it collects debris, chemicals, sediment, and other pollutants that can seriously impair water quality. On the ground, rainwater mixes with these pollutants to create natural and human-made pollutants, which can include contaminants such as:

❖ Oil, grease, metals, and coolants from vehicles

❖ Fertilizers, pesticides, and other chemicals from farms, gardens, and homes

❖ Bacteria from pet wastes and failing septic systems

❖ Soil from construction sites and other bare ground

❖ Detergents from car and equipment washing

❖ Accidental spills, leaky storage containers, and whatever else ends up on the ground

The polluted runoff then rushes into nearby gutters and storm drains, where it is commonly conveyed through Municipal Separate Storm Sewer Systems (MS4s) and eventually discharged into streams, lakes, rivers, bays, and oceans—the same bodies of water we use for swimming, fishing, and drinking water. In many areas, stormwater runoff enters vital surface waters without treatment, conveying contaminants that were collected along the way. Stormwater is a major contributor to urban nonpoint source pollution.

NONPOINT SOURCE POLLUTION

Nonpoint source pollution results from stormwater and snowmelt carrying and depositing contaminants into surface and ground waters. Nonpoint source pollution is detrimental to fresh water supplies, often contaminating drinking water sources and adversely affecting the health of plants, fish, animals, and people. Excess volumes of runoff from impervious surfaces also cause stream scouring, causing significant property damage as well as loss of aquatic habitat and floodplain connectivity.

Stormwater runoff is a cause of nonpoint source pollution; it contaminates the waterways that we use for swimming, fishing, and even drinking water supplies.

Section 2. The Role of Trees in Stormwater Management

In nature, trees play critical roles in controlling stormwater runoff and protecting surface waters from sediment and nutrient loading. In cities, trees can play an important role in stormwater management by reducing the amount of runoff that enters stormwater and combined sewer systems. Trees, acting as mini-reservoirs, control stormwater at the source.

A healthy urban forest can reduce runoff in the following ways:

❖ **Transpiration**—Trees draw large quantities of water from the soil for use in photosynthesis. The water is eventually released into the atmosphere as vapor from the canopy, a process termed transpiration.

❖ **Interception**—Leaves, branches, and trunk surfaces intercept and absorb rainfall, reducing the amount of water that reaches the ground, delaying the onset and reducing the volume of peak flows.

❖ **Reduced Throughfall**—Tree canopies reduce soil erosion by diminishing the volume and velocity of rainfall as it falls through the canopy, lessening the impact of raindrops on barren surfaces.

❖ **Increased Infiltration**—Root growth and decomposition increase soil infiltration capacity and rate.

❖ **Phytoremediation**—Along with water, trees take up trace amounts of harmful chemicals, including metals, organic compounds, fuels, and solvents from the soil. Inside the tree, these chemicals may be transformed into less harmful substances, used as nutrients and/or stored in roots, stems, and leaves.

TREES CAN BE MORE THAN JUST LANDSCAPING

While trees have long been recognized for their ability to help clean the air, reduce energy needs, raise property values, and mitigate heat island effects, their innate ability to absorb and divert rainfall has been underutilized. Trees have proven value in reducing runoff and mitigating the costs of stormwater management. In fact, research by the United States Forest Service has shown the environmental and economical values trees contribute to the community.

The United States Forest Service software suite, i-Tree, provides urban forestry analysis and benefit assessment tools. Specific to stormwater management are the i-Tree applications Streets and Hydro. i-Tree Streets was developed to estimate the environmental and economical impacts street trees have on a community. i-Tree Hydro was designed to simulate the effects of tree and impervious cover changes on stream flow and water quality within a defined watershed.

In 2010, the State of Indiana Department of Natural Resources conducted a statewide street tree benefit study using i-Tree Streets. The study showed that Indiana's street trees returned a multitude of environmental services and economic benefits annually to the community, including services that conserved energy ($9.7 million), managed stormwater ($24.1 million), improved air quality ($2.8 million), and sequestered carbon dioxide ($1.1 million). Less tangible, but equally significant, the aesthetic and social benefits and increased property values gained because of the presence of street trees were estimated at $41 million dollars per year to Indiana communities.

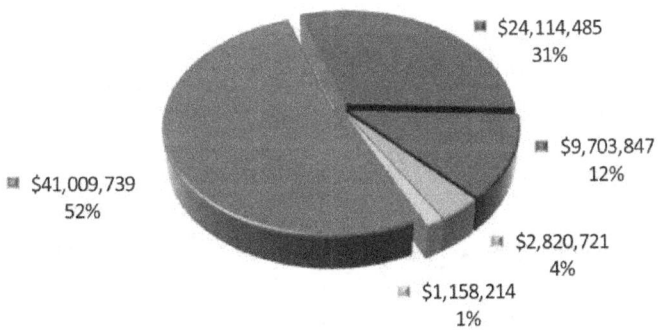

■ $24,114,485
31%

■ $9,703,847
12%

■ $41,009,739
52%

■ $2,820,721
4%

■ $1,158,214
1%

■ Aesthetic/Other   ■ Stormwater   ■ Energy   ■ Air Quality   ■ CO$_2$

Figure 1. Environmental and economic benefits extrapolated for 567 Indiana communities using i-Tree Streets. http://www.itreetools.org/resources/reports/ Indiana_Statewide_Street_Tree_Analysis.pdf viewed 11 May, 2011.

For the 23 communities involved in this statewide project, street trees provided approximately $30 million of functional benefits each year. Applied to all 567 Indiana communities, the annual benefits afforded by street trees were nearly $79 million (Figure 1). Reductions in stormwater management costs accounted for 64% of the environmental services (stormwater, energy, air quality, and CO$_2$) provided by street trees.

i-Tree Streets studies performed in communities of all sizes in every ecoregion show a similar savings trend in stormwater management costs because of the presence of street trees. Using trees to help manage stormwater, other than just for landscaping, significantly reduces stormwater management costs, as well as provides other valuable environmental services such as improvements in air quality and reductions in carbon dioxide.

DESIGN SITES FOR SUCCESS

To effectively use trees for the management of stormwater runoff, the site must be designed properly. Site design is critical to the success of any project, even when the project seems as simple as planting a tree. Urban trees require space, proper soil, drainage, and irrigation. Soil properties and soil volume are keys to growing trees in urban landscapes and using them successfully as a means to managing runoff.

A soil's porosity (amount of available pore space), permeability (how interconnected pore spaces are), and infiltration rate (how quickly the water moves through the soil) are critical to the success of a street tree and its ability to absorb stormwater. These soil properties affect the amount of air, moisture, and nutrients that are available in the root zone and how much runoff is absorbed into the ground instead of flowing over the ground.

Impervious surfaces and compacted soils in urban areas create challenges for both stormwater managers and urban foresters by preventing the infiltration of runoff into the ground. One way to address these problems, providing a solution for both, is to design tree planting areas to increase infiltration and limit compaction, and engineer them to receive and process street and rooftop runoff.

Designing the tree planting to accommodate the largest size tree possible will increase its stormwater utility function. Big trees with their large, dense canopies manage the most stormwater, and should be considered where the location is appropriate

GROW BIGGER TREES TO REDUCE MORE RUNOFF

Engineering a tree planting area which enables trees to grow to their full size, and where space allows to grow big trees, takes planning. Big trees require large volumes of soil and aboveground and belowground space to grow. Much research has been done to determine the relationship between soil volume and mature tree size. And although no universal standard for soil volume requirements for expected mature tree size exists in arboriculture, it is generally accepted that a large-sized tree (16 inches diameter at breast height) needs at least 1,000 cubic feet of uncompacted soil (Figure 2).

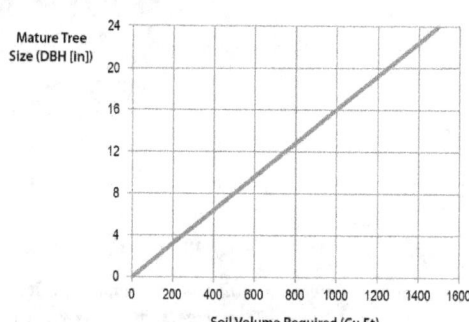

Figure 2. James Urban (1992) synthesized data from Bassuk and Lindsey (1991) and others to determine a relationship between soil volume requirements and mature tree size. The larger the tree, the more soil volume it needs.

6

A tree's ability to establish, grow to its full potential, and remain healthy is largely dependent upon soil volume. If too little soil is available, the tree will not reach full stature, regardless of what species of tree is planted. Trees without adequate soil volume tend to be short-lived and don't function as useful components of a city's infrastructure. Poorly designed sites—those lacking adequate soil and space—generally require continual, costly plant healh care and often continual replantment of trees. Designing a site for success—providing both soil and space—will grow the biggest tree the site can accommodate and, thus, divert and absorb the most stormwater (Figure 3).

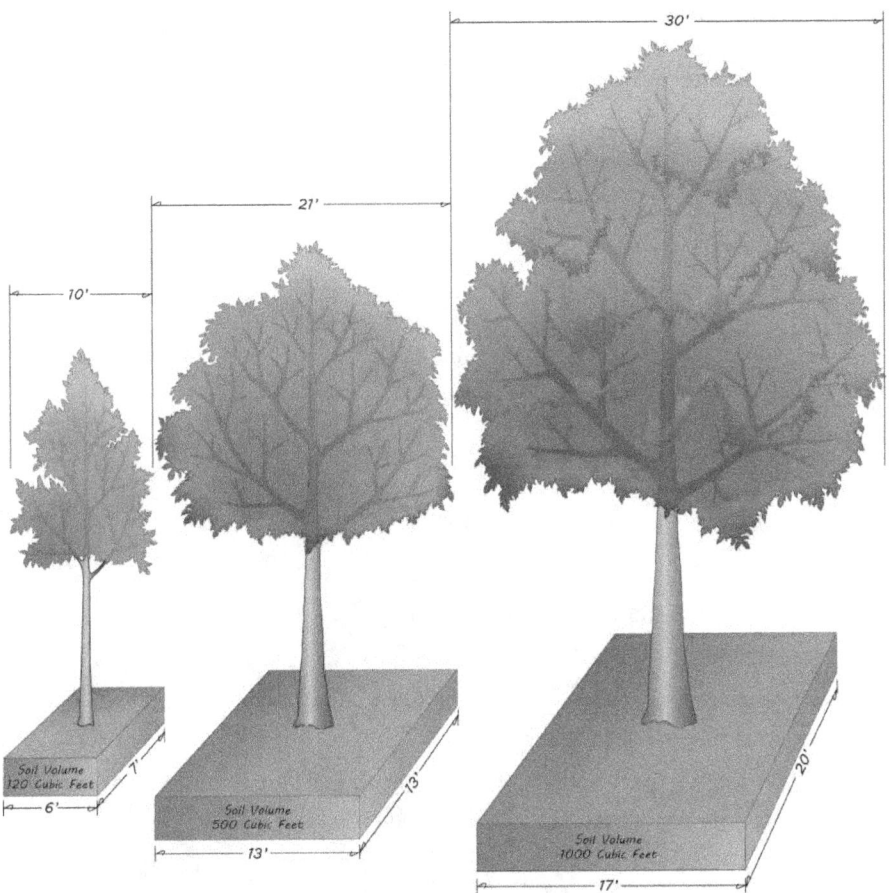

Figure 3. Tree growth is limited by soil volume. To grow big trees, large amounts of uncompacted soil are needed. For a mature tree with a canopy spread of approximately 30 feet, 1,000 cubic feet of soil is needed. Illustration from Casey Trees, 2008.

STREET TREE DESIGN FAILURES

Streetscape designs and even individual tree planting spaces often fail to address the needs of trees. Common design failures include compacted soil, improper (too small) tree pit size, a lack of soil for root growth, and impervious surfaces directly above the tree. Compaction—under the entire extent of the tree canopy—destroys soil porosity and permeability, limiting water infiltration and tree root growth. A tree pit that is too small and lacks the needed soil volume is inadequate for growing trees to their full potential, or even sustaining them for more than a decade. A tree placed in an area that lacks space and soil and regular access to rainfall or stormwater are destined for failure. Impervious surfaces cause stormwater to run off the site, preventing infiltration and forcing tree roots to grow towards the surface in search of air and moisture. This often results in the common problem of sidewalk upheaval as roots grow upward to reach all important oxygen and water.

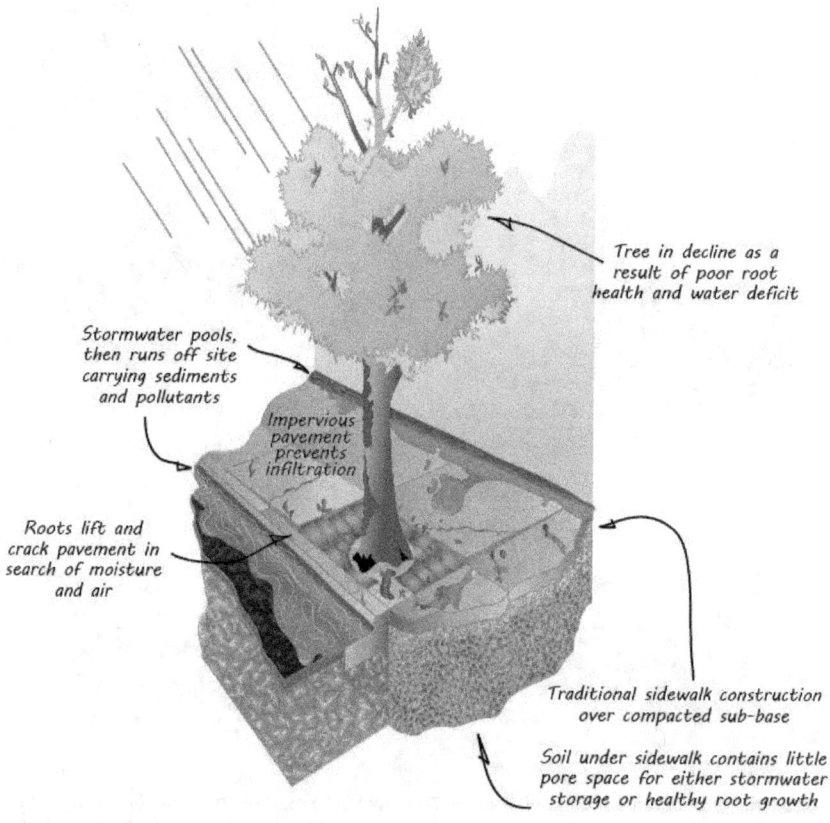

Tree in decline as a result of poor root health and water deficit

Stormwater pools, then runs off site carrying sediments and pollutants

Impervious pavement prevents infiltration

Roots lift and crack pavement in search of moisture and air

Traditional sidewalk construction over compacted sub-base

Soil under sidewalk contains little pore space for either stormwater storage or healthy root growth

Eventually, and because of poor root health due to site design failures, a tree shows signs of decline and may present an increased risk of limb or tree failure and liability. Often these declining trees are removed because the tree was a problem; however, in reality, it was the site design that was the problem, not the tree. The cost of removing and replacing this tree—a significant investment—is a waste of a community's money and time and it could have been prevented with proper design.

IN A WELL-DESIGNED SYSTEM, YOUR STREET TREES CAN…

With proper design, street trees can grow to their full size and live for many decades, enhancing streetscapes and providing stormwater utility services to the community.

Well-designed street tree systems are being achieved in even the most challenging urban environments. Creative designs are engineered to provide both space for trees to grow and for stormwater to be managed. Pavements can be supported by pillars, piles, and structural cells, allowing for large volumes of uncompacted soil below ground. Structural soils are engineered to be compactable enough to support some vehicle traffic, yet the gravel with a soil media adhered to the stone provides porosity and enough soil for healthy root growth. Surface treatments that are permeable with inlets provided to increase infiltration into the soil profile can enhance tree survival and manage runoff. Above- and belowground storage areas can be created and fed by downspouts and curb inlets to increase capacity and holding time. Overflow pipes direct excess flows from large storms to high-flow management systems.

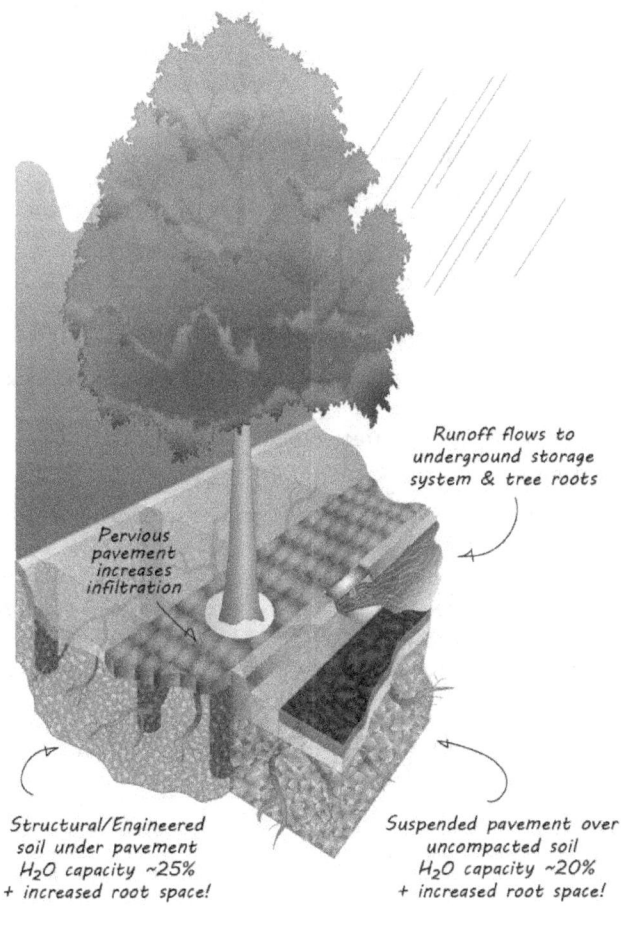

Runoff flows to underground storage system & tree roots

Pervious pavement increases infiltration

Structural/Engineered soil under pavement
H_2O capacity ~25%
+ increased root space!

Suspended pavement over uncompacted soil
H_2O capacity ~20%
+ increased root space!

When tree planting areas are designed and engineered with healthy trees as a goal, not an afterthought, trees grow to their maximum size, extending dense canopies and provide the greatest stormwater utility benefits to our cities, as well as other environmental and economic benefits including:

- ❖ **Improving Air Quality.** Trees absorb gaseous pollutants including ozone and nitrogen dioxide; intercept particulate matter such as dust, smoke, and pollen; and increase oxygen levels.
- ❖ **Saving Energy.** Shade from tree canopies reduces heat island effects; transpiration cools the air by adding moisture.
- ❖ **Increasing Property Values.** Trees provide beauty, privacy, and a sense of place.
- ❖ **Reducing Carbon Dioxide (CO_2).** Trees reduce CO_2 directly by sequestration and indirectly by lowering the demand for energy.
- ❖ **Providing Socioeconomic Benefits.** Trees can reduce crime (Kuo and Sullivan, 2001), speed up recovery time (Ulrich, 1984 and 1986), and improve perceptions of business districts (Wolf, 2000).
- ❖ **Protecting Water Quality.** Trees protect water quality by filtering and reducing stormwater runoff.

Urban trees can grow big and provide more than beauty and shade to a city. Engineered tree planting areas that provide the soil volume needed for tree growth and integrate with stormwater infrastructure for increased runoff management are being used in cities throughout the country to control stormwater and reduce runoff. Photo courtesy of Davey Resource Group.

In cities around the world and in every ecoregion in the United States, street trees are providing measurable environmental benefits. Their innate ability to capture stormwater reduces the load on existing stormwater management systems, which in turn reduces treatment costs as well as the need for additional facilities. The following table, using data from the United States Forest Service i-Tree Streets Reference Cities, illustrates just how much rainfall trees intercept and the savings to cities in stormwater management costs because of them.

Year Completed	i-Tree Reference City	Number of Trees Studied	Annual Stormwater Benefits (dollars)	Rainfall Intercepted Annually by Trees (million gallons)
2006	Albuquerque, N.M.	4,586	$55,833	11.1
2005	Berkeley, Calif.	36,485	$215,645	53.9
2004	Bismarck, N.D.	17,821	$496,227	7.1
2007	Boise, Idaho	23,262	$96,238	19.2
2005	Boulder, Colo.	25,281	$357,255	44.9
2006	Charleston, S.C.	15,244	$171,406	28.3
2005	Charlotte, N.C.	85,146	$2,077,393	209.5
2004	Cheyenne, Wyo.	17,010	$55,301	5.7
2003	Fort Collins, Colo.	31,000	$403,597	37.4
2005	Glendale, Ariz.	21,480	$18,198	1.0
2007	Honolulu, Hawaii	235,800	$350,104	35.0
2008	Indianapolis, Ind.	117,525	$1,977,467	318.9
2005	Minneapolis, Minn.	198,633	$9,071,809	334.8
2007	New York City, N.Y.	592,130	$35,628,220	890.6
2009	Orlando, Fla.	68,211	$539,151	283.7
2003	San Francisco, Calif.	2,625	$466,554	99.2
2001	Santa Monica, Calif.	29,229	$110,784	3.2

Street trees in cities throughout America make a difference in the amount of runoff entering combined sewer systems and stormwater drains. The mere presence of street trees reduces runoff by millions of gallons and saves cities tens of thousands to millions of dollars annually in stormwater management facility costs. Data from the United States Forest Service i-Tree Streets Reference Cities Guides are available at: http://www.fs.fed.us/psw/programs/uesd/uep/tree_guides.php.

Section 3. Stormwater Management Systems with Trees

SUSPENDED PAVEMENT AND STRUCTURAL CELLS

In a suspended pavement or structural cell system, pavement or the intended ground surface is supported by a network of pillars, piles, or structural cells. The suspension system supports the weight and forces of the pavement above and allows the soil below to remain uncompacted, accommodating tree roots and filtering and managing stormwater runoff. Suspended pavement can accommodate large volumes of soil needed for big tree growth.

Depending on engineering and design, suspended pavement and structural cells can support varying surface loads, including vehicular.

Practices: new construction/redevelopment/retrofit.

Applications: streetscapes, green streets, plazas, parking areas, green roofs, and tree pits and lawns.

Suspended pavement/structural cell system (black pillars above) supports pavement, creating large subsurface areas of uncompacted soil for root growth, bioremediation, and storage of stormwater.

How Suspended Pavement Benefits Stormwater Management and Trees

Soil Volume. Large volumes of soil are needed for tree growth—this system does that well.

Load Bearing. Can be engineered to meet loading standards, including some vehicles.

Bioremediation. Soil, roots, and soil biota filter stormwater, removing trace amounts of harmful chemicals including metals, organic compounds, fuels, and solvents.

Helps Trees Grow. Field studies found that trees in uncompacted, suspended pavement systems had better color, more root growth, and grew faster and larger than most other treatments, including structural soil (Smiley et al., 2006).

Transpiration. Stormwater is dissipated by trees through transpiration. Since this system actually gets stormwater to the tree roots, more transpiration can occur.

Tree Preservation. Existing trees can be preserved by suspending pavement over lateral roots.

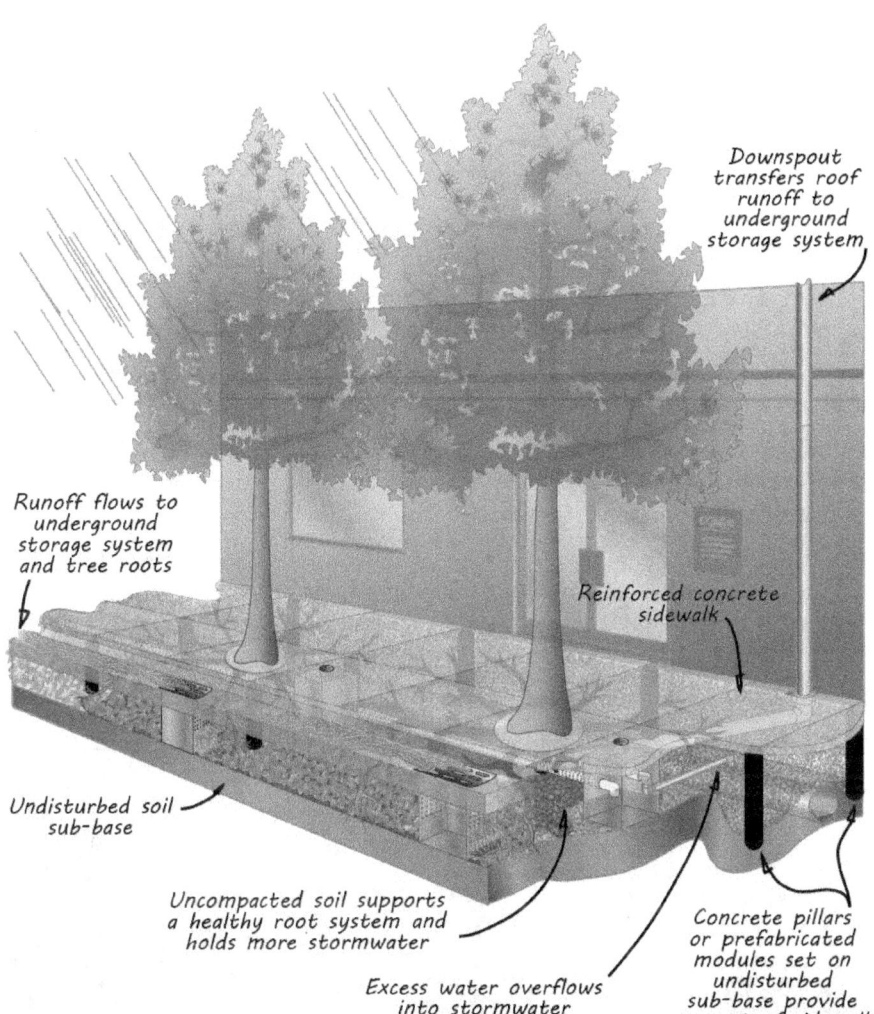

Downspout transfers roof runoff to underground storage system

Runoff flows to underground storage system and tree roots

Reinforced concrete sidewalk

Undisturbed soil sub-base

Uncompacted soil supports a healthy root system and holds more stormwater

Excess water overflows into stormwater distribution pipe

Concrete pillars or prefabricated modules set on undisturbed sub-base provide support of sidewalk over uncompacted soil layer

World Trade Center Memorial Plaza

Designed by Michael Arad and Peter Walker and Partners, a California-based landscape architecture company, the World Trade Center Memorial Plaza was designed to be one of the most sustainable green plazas ever built. The Memorial will feature approximately 400 swamp white oak and sweet gum trees planted using a suspended pavement system. The memorial is designed to collect the stormwater that falls into tanks below the plaza surface. The stormwater storage potential will exceed the irrigation needs of the plaza so daily and monthly irrigation requirements for the trees will be met by the harvested stormwater.

Engineered designs should include drainage and inlet and outlet locations along with elevations.

Overflow outlets are needed to prevent flooding.

Since suspended pavement sits on top of a sub-base, underdrains may be beneficial if the underlying surface is impervious and tends to pond water. Ponding water may suffocate trees.

Grasses, permeable pavers or pavements, and other surface treatments are appropriate for use with the system.

Underground utilities can be placed around and even through suspended pavement systems. However, all underground utilities should be protected from water and root penetration.

For system repair or utility access requiring excavation of suspended sections, to date, backfilling with soil, structural soil, or other aggregate has been done where the suspended pavement removed cannot be replaced.

Build the system large enough to grow many trees and manage a desired amount of runoff or storm event. A few structural cells or strips of suspended pavement may be good enough for growing a tree, but to manage stormwater runoff, contiguous areas of suspended pavement interconnected with other green and grey infrastructure is needed.

Consult engineers and landscape architects for design and arborists for tree specifications.

Structural cell installation in an urban streetscape; frames and decks pictured (below). Completed installation showing trees growing in the structural cell system (right). Photos courtesy of Deep Root Partners, L.P.

STRUCTURAL SOIL

Structural soil refers to a group of soil-on-gravel mixes that are designed to support tree growth and serve as a sub-base for pavements. Structural soils are highly porous, engineered aggregate mixes designed to be used under asphalt and concrete pavements as the load-bearing and leveling layer. In addition to providing a compactable base for pavements, structural soil provides a soil component (*i.e.*, engineered dirt) to the aggregate mix that facilitates root growth—common road bases do not have this tree-friendly component.

Structural soils are typically composed of 70% to 80% angular gravel and 20% to 30% clay loam soil and a small amount of hydrogel (~3%) to prevent separation during mixing. Structural soils have 20% to 25% void space which supports root growth and accommodates stormwater runoff.

Structural soil (grey stones above) is compactable to some roadway base standards yet provides pore space and soil for root growth and the storage of stormwater.

Practices: new construction/redevelopment/retrofit.

Conceptual diagram of structural soil (Bassuk, 2007)

Applications: streets, streetscapes, green streets, plazas, parking areas, green roofs, and tree planting areas, and tree pits and lawns.

How Structural Soil Benefits Stormwater Management and Trees

Load Bearing. Structural soil can be compacted to meet load-bearing requirements, and can even support some roadways, while preserving porosity and permeability.

Reduces Runoff—Manages Stormwater. The aggregate mix has void space that accommodates runoff.

Helps Trees Grow. Structural soils provide pore space for tree roots and a clay loam or climate-specific soil component that supports tree growth. The high volume of rock may preclude a large tree from growing to full size; however, continued fertilization of the tree will enhance the aggregate mix with nutrients and promote growth.

Stormwater Storage. A reservoir can be created underneath pavements to store runoff and desired storm events, shaving peak flows and reducing overall volume of runoff.

Infiltration. Structural soils have high porosity that allows tree roots to penetrate it freely, and stormwater to infiltrate it rapidly.

Easy Tree Planting. Trees are planted as they would be in normal soil. A 24-inch to 36-inch reservoir depth is generally considered optimal for tree growth, storing 6.25 to 9.36 inches of rain, respectively (Bassuk, 2007).

Multi-tasking. When planting tree grow spaces, structural soil can rise to surface grade, acting as a groundcover, maximizing opportunities for infiltration, aeration, and transpiration.

pH and Stone Type

Trees are sensitive to pH (acidity or alkalinity). pH can significantly affect the life and health of a tree and its ability to absorb nutrients. When using structural soil, the pH of the soil and water will be influenced by the type of stone used in the mix, whether limestone, granite, lava rock, or other stone. In systems that incorporate concrete products, the pH will continue to rise over time as concrete deteriorates. Always plant tree species that are compatible with the growing environment's and structural soil's pH.

In some cases, the addition of chemicals may be necessary to help offset pH conditions. These chemicals should be selected so as to not damage the concrete or other materials. Designs should consider this aspect of long-term maintenance and try to minimize these effects.

Design Considerations

Because structural soils are only 20% to 30% soil, large volumes may be needed to provide sufficient resources for trees (Loh et al., 2003).

A proper gravel gradation is critical for road base applications. Testing by pavement and geotechnical engineers is necessary and ensures soundness.

The sub-grade may need to be compacted and be impermeable to meet the installation's overall requirements for traffic loading, etc. In this case, a sub-drain system between the structural soil and compacted sub-grade is necessary to prevent standing water that could suffocate the tree roots.

Typical structural soil streetscape installation (above). Trees growing in structural soil in high-use area (below). Photos courtesy of Dr. Nina Bassuk, Urban Horticulture Institute, Cornell University.

When structural soil is being used as a reservoir for stormwater, the sub-soil may become saturated at times, resulting in lower soil strength. Consult a geotechnical engineer to determine if a separation geotextile is necessary.

Lateral flow through structural soil is extremely rapid. If the sub-base is permeable, or has some permeable areas, throughflow is likely to be fast. If surrounding areas are impermeable, ponding is possible. Provide overflow and underdrain outlets as needed.

Suppliers of structural soil should ensure that the mix used has the correct soil-to-gravel ratio, stone composition, and size and shape for the site and ecoregion.

For roads and other surfaces intended to support vehicular use, measure the bearing capacity of the structural soil used to ensure it meets regional Department of Transportation standards.

Build the system large enough to grow many trees and manage a desired amount of runoff or storm event. A few areas or strips of structural soil may be good enough for growing a tree, but to manage stormwater runoff, contiguous areas of structural soil interconnected with other green and grey infrastructure is needed.

Consult engineers and landscape architects for design and arborists for tree specifications.

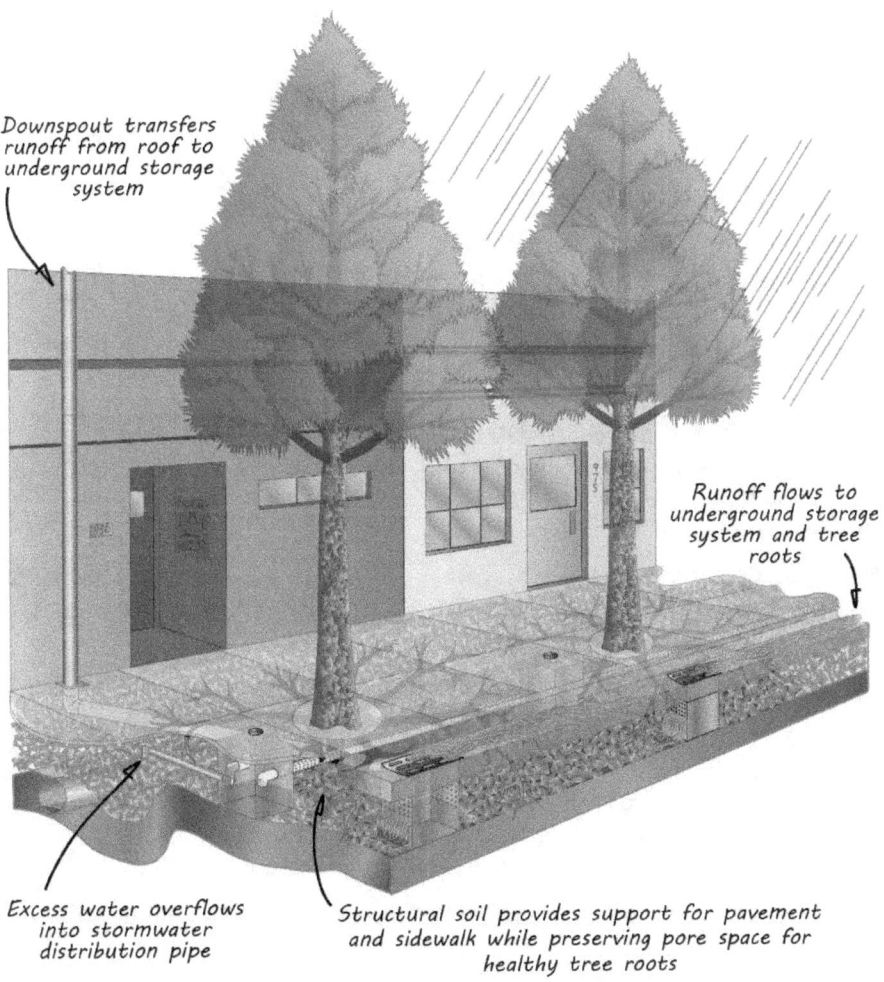

Downspout transfers runoff from roof to underground storage system

Runoff flows to underground storage system and tree roots

Excess water overflows into stormwater distribution pipe

Structural soil provides support for pavement and sidewalk while preserving pore space for healthy tree roots

STORMWATER TREE PITS

Street trees provide natural stormwater management. When tree pits provide enough uncompacted soil volume to grow large-sized trees, they become an integral part of stormwater management. Trees act as mini-reservoirs absorbing, diverting, and purifying rainfall on the spot. While tree pits can be individual, connecting multiple tree pits by soil paths or drains can increase soil volume for both trees and stormwater management opportunities.

Stormwater tree pits are similar to traditional street tree pits except they are modified to have increased growing space, be interconnected, and receive and treat stormwater runoff. Stormwater benefits increase with the number of stormwater tree pits installed and connected.

Practices: new construction/redevelopment/ retrofit.

Applications: tree lawns, medians, plazas, streetscapes, parking areas, green roofs, and green streets.

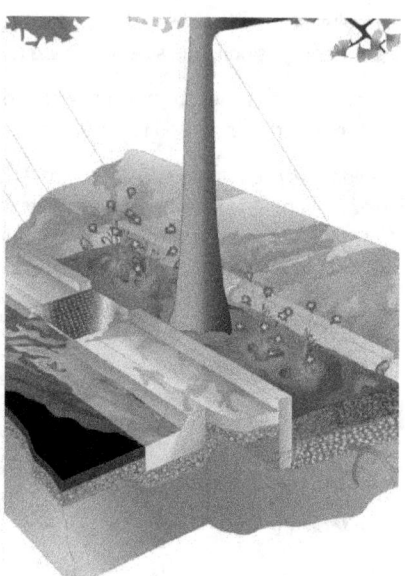

Stormwater tree pits are designed to increase infiltration through inlets and pervious surfaces. Trees transpire water, reducing the amount of water entering constructed runoff management systems.

How Stormwater Tree Pits Benefit Stormwater Management and Trees

Reduces Runoff—Manages Stormwater. The connection between tree pits and the integration of other grey and green stormwater management systems reduces runoff and increases the amount of stormwater managed.

Helps Trees Grow. Stormwater tree pits have additional soil volume and grow space, regular irrigation, and improved drainage. Compared to most traditional tree pits, they provide an improved growing environment for trees.

Bioremediation. Soil, roots, and soil biota filter stormwater, removing trace amounts of harmful chemicals including metals, organic compounds, fuels, and solvents.

Design Considerations

Stormwater tree pits are constructed similar to traditional street tree pits, but are engineered to accept and treat runoff. A continuous soil trench, drains, or other grey or green infrastructure should connect individual tree pits, maximizing capacity.

Stormwater tree pits are useful in streetscape retrofits when existing soils are very compacted or poor and underground space is limited.

Can be installed in conjunction with repair of underground utilities or streetscape retrofits.

Tree species selection is critical for stormwater tree pits. Plant trees that are adapted to soil and site conditions. Arborists should be consulted for tree specifications.

Directing runoff into grow spaces and tree pits with grading, inlets, and pervious surfaces can maximize infiltration and reduce stormwater runoff.

Connect enough stormwater tree pits to manage a desired amount of runoff or storm event. A few stormwater tree pits may be good enough for growing trees along a street, but to manage stormwater runoff, contiguous strips of stormwater tree pits interconnected with other green and grey infrastructure are needed.

Consult engineers and landscape architects for design. As with other designs, overflows and ponding require management.

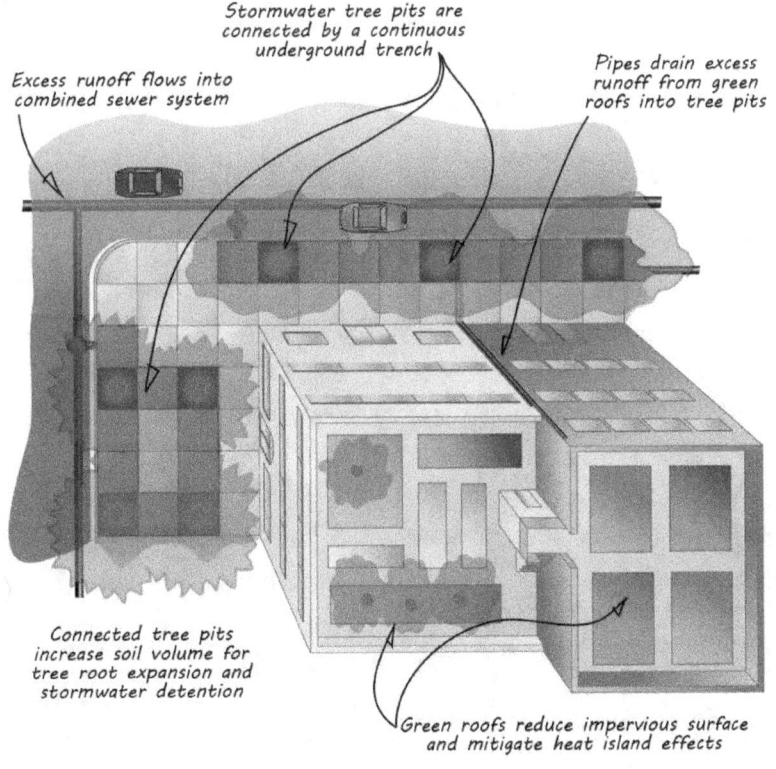

Stormwater tree pits are connected by a continuous underground trench

Excess runoff flows into combined sewer system

Pipes drain excess runoff from green roofs into tree pits

Connected tree pits increase soil volume for tree root expansion and stormwater detention

Green roofs reduce impervious surface and mitigate heat island effects

PERMEABLE PAVEMENTS

Permeable pavement refers to a wide variety of surfaces, including concretes, asphalts, and various types of grid and paver systems, that allow for rapid infiltration of water. Permeable pavement has a network of voids or spaces that allow water to pass through. Installations typically include a belowground, load-bearing stone reservoir that can store runoff until it percolates and interflows through the subsurface.

When combined with other engineered systems that promote tree growth, such as structural soil, suspended pavement, and stormwater tree pits, the volume of runoff infiltrating into the system can be increased significantly and tree growth maximized.

Permeable pavements (surface shown above) increase infiltration, allowing more runoff to be absorbed and available for use by the tree.

Practices: new construction/redevelopment/ retrofit.

Applications: curbs, cutouts, sidewalks, plazas and parking areas, and low-traffic areas.

How Permeable Pavement Benefits Stormwater Management and Trees

Infiltration. Reduces impervious surface. Rainfall enters the ground directly, almost where it falls. May reduce or eliminate the requirement for land for stormwater ponds.

Reduces Runoff—Manages Stormwater. Permeable surface reduces runoff.

Filtration. Some permeable pavements eventually build up a film of biomass that naturally reduces trace amounts of hydrocarbons, nitrogen, and other biodegradable pollutants.

Recycled. Many pavers and pavements are manufactured using recycled materials.

Helps Trees Grow. Increases the amount of oxygenated water directly entering the root zone, improving tree health.

Tree Preservation. Can be used around trees where a load-carrying surface is required.

Reduces Puddling. Because water freely drains through the pavement, water is less likely to accumulate on the surface of the pavement.

Design Considerations

Proper design, construction, and maintenance is required to reduce clogging and failure.

Do not seal or repave with non-permeable materials as these clog the surface and prevent the pavement from allowing water to infiltrate.

Vacuuming of debris is recommended to ensure void spaces do not clog. Sweeping can push debris into the void spaces.

Permeable pavement allows stormwater to infiltrate surface, recharging sub-soil and irrigating trees

Aggregate layer provides temporary storage while stormwater infiltrates sub-soil

Sub-soil

Do not cover the surface with toxic materials as they will pollute the underlying soils and water.

Sand is not recommended as joint filler for pervious, interlocking concrete paver (PICP) systems. Sand is a growing medium that will support mold, moss, and other vegetation, which can render the surface impervious.

Avoid installing in areas where activities generate sediment or contaminated runoff. Areas where sand is applied should not be considered for permeable pavement installations.

A common failure of permeable pavement is sediment accumulation during construction. Ensure that the surrounding construction area is completely stabilized before installing permeable pavements.

Proper jointing for contraction and expansion is required.

Snow plows must avoid surface contact.

Consult engineers and landscape architects for appropriate design and arborists for tree specifications.

Permeable pavements increase infiltration, helping trees receive oxygenated water and reduce stormwater runoff. When used in conjunction with other engineered systems designed to grow big trees and manage stormwater, permeable pavements can boost the infiltration rate and amount of runoff entering the system. Photo courtesy of Davey Resource Group.

Other Vegetated Systems Designed to Mimic Nature

Stormwater management systems designed to mimic natural areas can be integrated into community, street, building, and even site developments to reduce the damaging effects of urbanization on rivers and streams and relieve pressures on combined sewer and stormwater systems. Bioswales, green streets, and green roofs are three such designed systems that incorporate a variety of green and grey infrastructure components to increase on-site infiltration and filtering of stormwater by natural processes. These created naturalistic systems disconnect flow from storm sewers and force runoff to areas such as landscaped planters, swales, and rain gardens. Vegetation, soils, and biota naturally filter stormwater while entry into grey infrastructure is delayed or even prevented.

These systems, even though they mimic nature, are usually complexly designed and can incorporate the engineered systems discussed in this guide.

FORESTED BIOSWALES

A bioswale is a graded depression designed to detain stormwater and promote infiltration. Stormwater is filtered by trees, vegetation, and soil biota.

To function properly, a bioswale should be constructed with a mix of soil, engineered or native, vegetation, and drainage. If the bioswale is surrounded by impervious surfaces, curbs, or barriers, it should be positioned to direct runoff into storage areas before slowly releasing it into storm drains. The swale takes advantage of a natural slope and reduces runoff speed. The vegetation in a swale reduces the "gullywasher" effect by absorbing some of the water as it moves downward. Check dams can be added along the length of the swale to slow runoff even more.

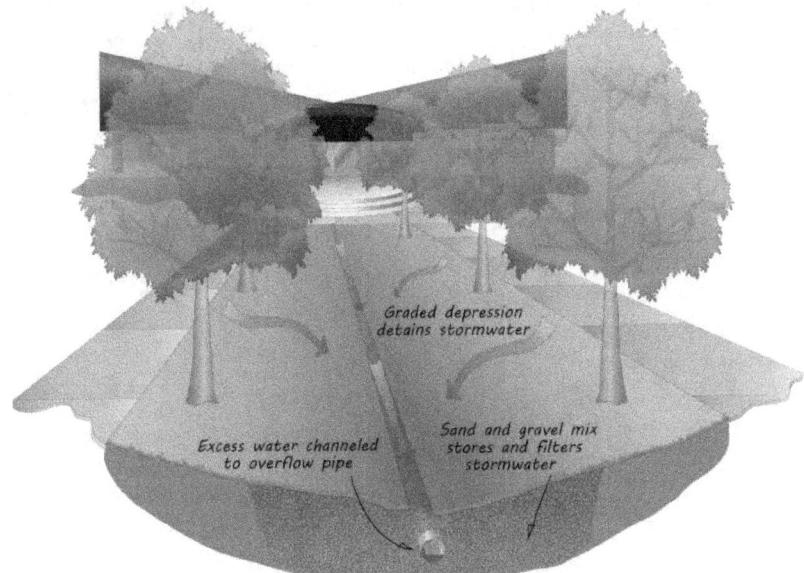

Graded depression
detains stormwater

Excess water channeled
to overflow pipe

Sand and gravel mix
stores and filters
stormwater

*Increased soil volume and vegetation, including trees, maximizes potential
for absorption, bioremediation, and phytoremediation*

GREEN ROOFS

Green roofs can be effectively used to reduce stormwater runoff from commercial, industrial, and residential buildings. In contrast to traditional asphalt or metal roofing, green roofs absorb, store, and later evapotranspire initial precipitation. Overflow is directed into stormwater and combined sewer systems.

A green roof manages stormwater on site through retention in the media. It reduces peak flow discharge to a stormwater sewer system. Its design requires a careful mix of impervious base materials to prevent leakage and support soils, plants, irrigation, and drainage systems, making it and the building below structurally sound and safe.

Green roofs reduce the amount of impervious surface and increase transpiration opportunities in even the densest urban cores. Photo courtesy of Davey Resource Group.

GREEN STREETS

A green street is designed to integrate a natural system of stormwater management within a public right-of-way. Green streets are generally planned to be visible components of a system of "green infrastructure" and are incorporated into the aesthetics of the community. Green streets make use of bioretention or bioswales and make the best use of the street tree canopy for stormwater interception as well as temperature mitigation and air quality improvement.

Green streets are an innovative way to manage stormwater on site and combat urban heat island effects. Photo courtesy of Davey Resource Group.

Green streets designs will vary from community to community or even street to street, but they all have the same goal—to reduce the amount of stormwater that directly enters into streams and rivers. The design and construction of a green street should be one component of a larger watershed approach to improving regional water quality.

Know the Rules

The engineered systems that use trees presented here are not applicable everywhere. When high concentrations of contaminants and/or pollutants are present in stormwater, infiltration may not be appropriate due to the risk of groundwater contamination, and the use of engineered systems may be regulated. Sites with very rocky soils, high bedrock, water tables less than four feet from the surface, limited drainage, and extreme slopes may not be suitable for increased infiltration rates common with the engineered systems presented. Sites with Karst geology run the risk of contaminating the groundwater. Before beginning a project, check and comply with local, state, and federal rules, regulations, codes, and other restrictions or mandates regarding the capture, manipulation, detention, and storage of stormwater.

References

Bassuk, Nina, Jason Grabosky, Ted Haffner, and Peter Trowbridge. 2007. Using Porous Asphalt and CU-Structural Soil. Cornell University, Ithaca, New York.

Casey Trees. 2008. Tree Space Design Growing the Tree Out of the Box. http://www.caseytrees.org/planning/design-resources/for-designers/tree-space/documents/TreeSpaceDesignReport.pdf. Viewed 14 July, 2010.

Indiana Department of Natural Resources (IDNR). http://www.itreetools.org/resources/reports/Indiana_Statewide_Street_Tree_ Analysis.pdf. Viewed 28 March, 2011.

Kuo, F., and W. Sullivan. 2001. Environment and Crime in the Inner City: Does Vegetation Reduce Crime? Environment and Behavior 33(3): 343–367.

Lindsey, Patricia and Nina Bassuk. 1991. Specifying soil volumes to meet the water needs of mature trees in containers. Journal of Arboriculture 17:141-149.

Loh, Felix, C.W., Jason C. Grabosky, and Nina L. Bassuk. 2003. Growth response of *Ficus benjamina* to limited soil volume and soil dilution in a skeletal soil container study. Urban Forestry & Urban Greening 2: 53-62.

Smiley, Thomas E., Lisa Calfee, Bruce R. Fraedrich, and Emma J. Smiley. 2006. Comparison of Structural and Noncompacted Soils for Trees Surrounded by Pavement. Arboriculture & Urban Forestry 32(4): 164-169.

Ulrich, R. 1986. Human Responses to Vegetation and Landscapes. Landscape and Urban Planning 13:29–44.

Ulrich, R. 1984. View through Window May Influence Recovery from Surgery. Science 224(4647): 420–421.

Urban, James R. 1992. Bringing order to the technical dysfunction within the urban forest. Journal of Arboriculture 18(2):85-90.

USGS. http://ga.water.usgs.gov/edu/watercycleevapotranspiration.html. Viewed 28 March, 2011.

Wolf, K. 2000. "Community Image - Roadside Settings and Public Perceptions." University of Washington College of Forest Resources, Factsheet #32.

Section 4. Case Studies

- ❖ Minneapolis, Minnesota: Structural Cells
- ❖ Charlotte, North Carolina: Suspended Pavement
- ❖ Ithaca, New York: Structural Soil
- ❖ Olympia, Washington: Structural Soil
- ❖ Chattanooga, Tennessee: Permeable Pavement

MINNEAPOLIS, MINNESOTA: STRUCTURAL CELLS

Year: 2010

Project Area: Marquette Avenue and 2nd Avenue (MARQ2).

Goals: Reshape transportation corridor and address capacity problem with urban stormwater runoff. Expect a 10% reduction in peak flows (peak storm event) to City's stormwater system based on modeling.

This downtown street project included installation of structural cells or tree cells to create conditions that promoted healthy mature trees and improved stormwater management in the core of the downtown district.

The project installed 173 trees along a new bus corridor using a modular system of structural cells that supported the sidewalk. The system created a void space that held 10 cubic feet of soil per unit (10,800 units were installed), allowing for existing or future utility pipes, protecting tree roots from compaction, and providing room for stormwater.

The system can temporarily hold large volumes of stormwater that will either be used by the trees (evapotranspiration) or will soak into the ground (infiltration).

Photos courtesy of Deep Root Partners, L.P.

Photo courtesy of Don McSween, City of Charlotte, North Carolina

Year: 1985

Project Area: Ten blocks of Tryon Street and two blocks of Trade Street; two of the major downtown thoroughfares.

Goals: Major renovation of downtown thoroughfares. City wanted large stately trees in its downtown area.

A custom, suspended pavement system using precast concrete pavement supported by earthen trench sidewalks was designed to promote tree growth in downtown Charlotte. This represents perhaps the lowest cost and simplest approach that may apply in construction where trench integrity can bear the load. The entire system was topped by nonpermeable pavers. The design included approximately 1,000 cubic feet of good usable soil per tree; 170 willow oaks (*Quercus phellos*) trees were planted.

In 2009, the willow oaks planted had an average diameter at breast height of 16 inches and an average height of 44 feet. In addition to growing big trees, the system modeled a 10% reduction in peak flows (peak storm event) to the City's stormwater system.

ITHACA, NEW YORK: STRUCTURAL SOIL

Year: 2005

Project Area: Parking lot, Ithaca, New York.

Goals: Improve tree growth, reduce runoff, and improve water quality in parking lots.

To show the benefits of the use of structural soil to grow trees, reduce runoff, and improve water quality in parking lots, a parking lot in Ithaca, NY was constructed using structural soil and a porous asphalt surface treatment. The entire parking lot was built over a 30-inch base of structural soil. Planting strips 3 feet by 18 feet were daylighted—cut into the asphalt—and bare root Accolade elms were planted directly into the structural soil base. The parking lot was designed to contain a 100-year rain event.

Photo courtesy of Dr. Nina Bassuk, Urban Horticulture Institute, Cornell University

OLYMPIA, WASHINGTON: STRUCTURAL SOIL

Year: 2001

Project Area: Downtown block, State Avenue.

Goals: Provide soil volume to grow trees in downtown areas and prevent sidewalk damage.

One hundred linear feet of sidewalk and existing soil to a depth of 36 inches were removed. Structural soil, trees in cut outs, and new sidewalks were installed.

Photo courtesy of Stacey Ray, City of Olympia, Washington

CHATTANOOGA, TENNESSEE: PERMEABLE PAVEMENT

Nonpermeable Concrete   Permeable Concrete

Photo courtesy of Gene Hyde, City of Chattanooga, Tennessee

Year: 1996

Project Area: Finley Stadium Parking Lot.

Goals: Control stormwater runoff and irrigate parking lot trees.

The former brownfield site was retrofit with sections of permeable concrete. An existing basement was re-purposed as a cistern to manage stormwater and grow big trees.

Approximately 40,000 square feet of permeable concrete was used. The pervious concrete accounts for approximately ⅓ of the parking lot. The entire system has perimeter drains for overflow. Runoff is intended to be harvested and stored in an underground cistern, which was essentially the waterproofed basement of a demolished building.

Additional Resources and Information

GREEN BUILDING

www.epa.gov/greenbuilding/

GREEN INFRASTRUCTURE

www.epa.gov/greeninfrastructure/

GREEN STREETS

www.epa.gov/owow_keep/podcasts/greenstreetsusa.html

GREENING

www.epa.gov/nps/lid

TECHNICAL GUIDE ASSISTANCE

For photograph, chart, or figure assistance, call 800-828-8312. Reference page number, title, and Stormwater to Street Trees guide.

U.S. Environmental Protection Agency

Office of Wetlands, Oceans and Watersheds

Nonpoint Source Control Branch (4503T)

1200 Pennsylvania Ave., NW

Washington, DC 20460

September 2013

EPA 841-B-13-001

www.ingramcontent.com/pod-product-compliance
Lightning Source LLC
Chambersburg PA
CBHW071019290526
45795CB00005B/1865